WHAT ARE THE WORLD'S GREATEST RACES?

SHIN☺Y
AND THE CHAOS CREW

Contents

Written by Rob Alcraft

Collins

What are the world's greatest races?

Let's find out! Is the greatest race the *fastest* or
the *longest* or the *strangest*? From **athletes** who train
for years, to people who race with cheese; from
the fastest animal racer to the slowest of snails –
everyone and everything is racing!

Who are the fastest humans?

The fastest humans over a short distance are sprinters. Some of these athletes can run 100 metres in under ten seconds.

SPEED CHECK

In a 100-metre race, the fastest human ever ran at 44.7 kilometres per hour.

Over long distances, such as a **marathon**, wheelchair athletes are the fastest. The very best non-disabled athletes can run a 42-kilometre marathon in about two hours. Wheelchair athletes are 40 minutes faster.

Are we getting faster?

Yes, we are! In 1922, the women's 100-metre record was 13.6 seconds. Today, it's 10.49 seconds – over three seconds faster.

What's the longest race?

This 4,989-kilometre-long marathon is the longest foot race. Competitors run 5,649 times round the same four streets in New York, USA. It takes around 52 days.

The runners wear out several pairs of trainers when taking part in this marathon.

What's the toughest race?

Swimming in open water is one of the toughest
forms of racing. One famous open-water race is
six kilometres across the Bosphorus Strait.
Competitors must battle currents and **tides** – as well
as everyone else.

the Bosphorus Strait, Turkey

How fast can a top cyclist go?

Racing cyclists keep up speeds of
40 kilometres per hour. Downhill, they can
reach speeds of 129 kilometres per hour.
That's faster than cars on a motorway.

What's the oldest race still going?

Dragon boats have been racing on Chinese rivers for over 2,500 years – making them the oldest racers.

RACER FACT

Dragon boats carry a drummer. The drumbeat keeps paddlers in time, and it is key to a boat's speed and success.

How fast does a race car go?

Formula One cars race at over 370 kilometres per hour. The cars could be built to go even faster, but they would come off the track at the bends!

RACER FACT

Formula One teams can change all four tyres on a race car in under two seconds.

This 1906 car won a long-distance race. Its average speed was just 23 kilometres per hour.

Can I drive a race car?

You can! Go-kart racing is a great way to try out motor racing.
The karts sit so close to the ground that racing feels like super-speed.

RACER FACT

The first go-karts used engines built to power chainsaws!

SPEED CHECK

Go-kart speed: 40+ kilometres per hour

What's the wackiest kind of motor racing?

A Demolition Derby is about as zany as racing cars can get. Competitors race old cars on a dirt track where crashing isn't just allowed – it's encouraged! The winner is the last car driving.

This sport is also called "banger racing".

What's the messiest race?

One of the messiest races is
the UK's Maldon Mud Race.
This is a dash through the oozy
River Blackwater. The record time
is 3.7 minutes, but it can take
half an hour to wade
through the 500 metres
of mud and slime.

SPEED CHECK
Mud runner: eight kilometres per hour

What's the greatest animal racer?

Pigeons are the superstars of animal racing. With the right winds, they travel at over 97 kilometres per hour in races of up to 1,600 kilometres. Their brain's internal **navigation** system means they always find their way home.

RACER FACT

Racing pigeons can sell for over one million pounds.

Which animals are the best team racers?

The ultimate team racers are sled dogs. In one of the longest races, teams of 14 dogs compete with their sled driver, called a musher, over a 1,500-kilometre course of ice and wilderness in Alaska, USA.

This is the Iditarod Trail Sled Dog Race.

RACER FACT

Dogs trained for racing can run as much as 11 hours a day.

SPEED CHECK

Dog speed: 10 to 24 kilometres per hour

OK then, what are the biggest animal racers?

Weighing in at over 1,000 kilograms, water **buffalo** are the hoofed giants of racing. Sprinting along faster than any human, buffalo races are a big event at festivals across Asia.

SPEED CHECK
Buffalo speed: 48 kilometres per hour

Where can I race my ostrich?

You can race ostriches in South Africa and the USA, where these two-metre tall, feathery racers are very popular. It's a bit like horse racing, but it's a lot harder to stay on an ostrich!

SPEED CHECK

Ostrich speed: 64 kilometres per hour

Can I really race in a pumpkin?

Of course you can! With a little hollowing out, giant pumpkins make brilliant racing craft. Just don't forget your paddle.

RACER FACT

The biggest pumpkin ever grown weighed more than a large moose!

What's the slowest race?

The slowest race is probably the Snail Racing World Championships, which take place in the British village of Congham. Sammy Snail – the current world champion – covered the traditional 13-inch (33-centimetre) race course in 2 minutes and 38 seconds.

SPEED CHECK

Snail speed: one mile (1.6 kilometres) in eight days

What's faster – a human or a cheese?

Cheese racing has taken place on a UK hillside
in Gloucestershire since at least 1826.
Usually the cheese is the fastest!

SPEED CHECK
Cheese speed: 113 kilometres per hour

cheese

There are so many great races!

Glossary

athletes experts at sport

buffalo a large cow-like animal used for milk and farm work

marathon a long-distance race of just over 42 kilometres

navigation finding and following a route

tides the twice daily rise and fall of the sea

Index

Pick a winner!

Who goes for the longest?

Which animal is the slowest?

Which animal is the fastest?

Whose race is the toughest?

22

Who goes furthest?

Which race is
the muddiest?

Who's fastest?

Which race do YOU think is the greatest?

Ideas for reading

Written by Christine Whitney
Primary Literacy Consultant

Reading objectives:
- discuss how items of information are related
- be introduced to non-fiction books that are structured in different ways
- discuss and clarify the meanings of words

Spoken language objectives:
- ask relevant questions
- speculate, imagine and explore ideas through talk
- participate in discussions

Curriculum links: Science: Animals, including humans; Writing: Write for different purposes

Word count: 944

Interest words: athletes, marathon, navigation, tides

Resources: pencils, crayons and paper

Build a context for reading
- Ask children to tell the group about a time when they were in a race. What type of race was it?
- Read the title of the book and ask children to discuss with each other what they think is the answer to the question. What types of races do they know? What would make *the greatest race*?
- Encourage children to name three things about the greatest races they would like to know. Keep these questions and see if they are answered by reading the book.

Understand and apply reading strategies
- Read page 4 and ask children to explain what they know about *sprinters*.
- Continue to read to page 7. Ask children to tell each other why the race across the Bosphorus Strait is called *the toughest race*. Suggest that they use the word *tides* in their answer.
- Read speed check facts on pages 15, 16 and 17. Which animal can run the fastest?